PARENTS' MANUAL

Silver Dolphin

San Diego, California

CONTENTS

Dear Parent,

Hearing the word "math" results in a variety of reactions. Many adults transfer their own learning experiences onto their children, resulting in a fear of this subject among children. Experience has taught us that previous methods of teaching math to children did not create enough understanding and interest.

This program will change your perception of math. You will be encouraged to join your child in being part of the new generation of mathematical entrepreneurs who can think, reason, strategize, and solve problems. The following key will lead the way through this program:

ATTITUDE
- A child's sincere desire to learn is at its optimum between the ages of 3 and 7 years.
- The foundation of all future learning is laid within this period.
- Attitude is the floor plan of the learning process.

SKILLS
- Learning will not take place without skills.
- Skills are the bricks, sand, and cement of the learning process.

KNOWLEDGE
- An enthusiastic child with a vibrant attitude acquires knowledge through the process of developing skills.
- Knowledge without skills will result in knowledge that cannot be applied.
- Knowledge that cannot be applied has the same value as no knowledge at all.

This program incorporates three simple steps of learning:
1. Concrete experiences
2. Semiconcrete representation
3. Abstract application

As a parent, it is essential for you to have a positive attitude toward the learning process. Encourage children by responding to their performance. Acknowledge their efforts as they progress. Never stop challenging them when higher achievement is possible.

A partnership with you, the parent, will assist children in obtaining the winning attitude needed to meet challenges. Through investigating and exploring, children will learn to solve problems and discover that math is magic.

Knowledge will be gained through understanding concepts and application will become as easy as child's play!

THREE STEPS OF LEARNING

Pointing out the differences between the three levels may make it easier to understand how your child will progress from one level to the next.

STEP 1: Concrete level (real objects)

- Concrete experiences are collected through the five senses. Through seeing, hearing, touching, tasting and smelling, the brain is being informed of what goes on around the body.
- Children store information from previous experiences in their brain.
  - ▸ They show their excitement when they hear the ice-cream truck.
  - ▸ They spit out food if they don't like the taste.
  - ▸ They hold up their fingers to show their age.
- Children cannot be taught what something tastes, smells, looks, sounds, or feels like if they don't have any experience references.

Visual:	Auditory:	Tactile:
The absorption of information through the eyes—that is, things that can be seen, such as activity books, storybooks, television, magazines, toys, and people.	The absorption of information through the ears—that is, things that can be heard, such as verbal communication, listening to the radio, recordings of stories, television, and toys with sounds.	The absorption of information through the sense of touch—that is, hands-on experiences such as feeling sand to understand the word *rough*, feeling a triangle to recognize three corners, putting cubes together to understand addition, and taking cubes away to understand subtraction.

- **Lead by example:** Parents who watch a lot of television raise children who are glued to television sets. Parents who read raise children who read. Parents who study raise children who study. There are exceptions, but children mostly follow in the footsteps of their mentors.
- **Provide challenging resources** that cater for visual, auditory, and tactile skill development. Information is retained if absorbed through these three senses simultaneously. The activity book in this program combines all three vital senses at the same time. Children use their tactile sense by building or constructing, while they follow the instructions (visual) and then have to answer to questions being asked (auditory). This is the best method to ensure that the information is stored in the long-term memory. (Absorption through one or two senses will usually cause the information to be stored for only a short time.)

STEP 2: Semiconcrete level (a picture of the object)

- At the semiconcrete level, children respond to a picture of the object.
- Although they don't have 8 counters, 8 bears, or 8 circles, they recognize the quantity of 8 when they see a picture of 8 objects.
- At this level, children should be given the opportunity to draw a picture or give their own representation of different quantities.

Step 3: Abstract level (words or numbers)

- Children are exposed to reading words and numbers.
- Children combine their understanding (concrete level) and their ability to represent their understanding with a drawing (semiconcrete level) by working with numbers and words comfortably and with true perception.

THREE STEPS OF LEARNING

CONCRETE:
A real thing or object

If children have their own dogs that they feed, stroke, and play with, they truly understand what the word *dog* means. It is not only the word that they understand, but they know and understand the implications and consequences of having a dog.

THIS LEVEL RESULTS IN UNDERSTANDING.

SEMICONCRETE:
A picture of something

When children have never physically taken care of a dog, but have learned about dogs from television or a computer, they have a distorted picture. They haven't fed or given water to a dog. They therefore have only a partial idea of what a dog is. The cause of this distortion is the lack of exposure to the real thing.

The same goes for math. The child has to deal with the concept before acting upon it.

MORE THAN HALF OF THE KNOWLEDGE IS LOST WHEN THE CONCRETE STAGE IS ABSENT.

ABSTRACT:
A written word or numeral

When a child has never seen a dog (not even a picture) and he has to read the word *dog* in a book, what would his understanding be?

The same will apply to math. Understand where it comes from, and then it is logical!

WHEN ANY CONCEPT IS INTRODUCED TO A CHILD ON AN ABSTRACT LEVEL ONLY, HE MAY RETAIN LESS THAN 20% UNDERSTANDING.

On a math level

Observe the steps for introducing a concept such as fractions:

CONCRETE:

Laying the foundation for fractions is a silent, concrete experience. Through variation, we repeat it in many modes without the child even knowing that this concept is being taught.

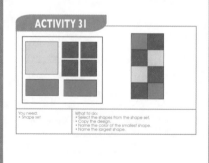

SEMICONCRETE:

In Grade 1, children advance to the semiconcrete level. At this point, the word *fraction* has not even been mentioned, but through semiconcrete activities where shapes are divided into equal pieces, the concept is being introduced.

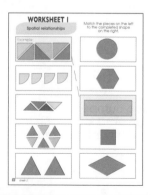

ABSTRACT:

Many educational systems do not include the first two levels or steps of learning. Attempts to teach fractions on an abstract level only result in confusion and frustration.

In Grade 2, this program continues to inculcate the concept before progressing to the abstract level.

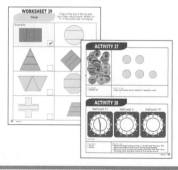

Components

- The activity book offers activities that require the use of the components in your math kit.
- Most children will have their own preferences and should be allowed some free play with the components before they are introduced to the activities.
- Allow them to unpack the components and discuss the shapes, colors, and sizes.
- Make sure that you introduce the correct names when using the components.

Shape set

The large yellow triangle has 3 sides, all of which are equal in length. All of the corners have the same angle.

The large green and small yellow triangles have 3 sides, of which only 2 sides are equal in length. Two of the corners have the same angle.

The large square is yellow and the smaller squares are blue. All 4 sides of a square are equal in length.

The rectangles are red. The rectangle has four sides and the opposite sides are equal in length.

The hexagon is blue. It has 6 sides and 6 corners.

The large circle is red and the small ones are blue.

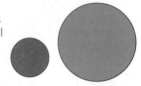

Bead set and lace

The bead colors are red, blue, green, and yellow.
The bead set has two of each shape in each of the four colors.
The beads can be threaded onto the lace.

Cube   Cylinder   Barrel   Sphere

Cube set

The cube set includes 20 cubes, with two in each of the following colors: red, blue, yellow, green, black, white, pink, purple, orange, and brown.

Cards

The deck consists of 26 number cards with pictures of objects or numerals. Thirteen of the cards have pictures of between one and thirteen objects. The rest of the cards are numbered from 1 to 13.

Spinner and templates

Included in the kit are a plastic spinner and three printed templates.

Plastic spinner

Shape template

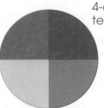
4-color template

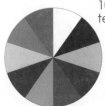
10-color template

ACTIVITY BOOK

Using the activity book

- It is advised that children start with Activity 1 and progress systematically through the book.
- If the child prefers, he may do the bead, shape, or cube activities in sequence.
- To utilize the program to its optimum, parents must ensure that children do not avoid activities that they dislike. A dislike usually indicates that the activity is challenging to the child and this is where the parent should become involved and assist.
- Children who struggle with threading usually need assistance with fine motor and eye-hand coordination skills.
- Children who struggle with the shape activities usually have a visual perception or spatial relationship problem that will improve through more exposure to shape designs.
- It is important to work at your child's pace—do not apply undue pressure.

Shape activities

- Selecting the correct shape means that children make a decision every time they choose a shape.
- Children must be alert and aware of the color and properties of each different shape.
- Some shapes have four sides (at this level squares and rectangles) but they are still different from each other.
- This set has three different triangles; children must select the correct color, size, and shape before applying it. This skill is called visual discrimination and is vital for reading, writing, and mathematics.
- The level of difficulty of the activities rises systematically to ensure optimum progression.
- A wide range of skills is covered.
- Shape activities test observation skills to the maximum. In some activities different shapes are combined to create new shapes. Sometimes children find it difficult to recognize the new shapes. Do not be discouraged—your child will succeed and also acquire the valuable skills of perseverance and problem solving.
- Encourage children to make their own designs and patterns.

Cube activities

- The cube activities are graded into various levels of difficulty.
- Children are challenged to select and sequence the cubes into the correct order.
- Reasoning and logical thinking are developed when the first cubes are joined to make the positioning of the next cube possible.
- Fine motor skills and eye-hand coordination will be practiced in every activity.
- One-to-one correspondence (the skill of observing an object or picture and repeating exactly what was observed) will be practiced when copying the activities.
- Children learn to master the concept of position with true understanding while progressing through the activities.
- Positional concepts (above, behind, on top, left, and right) are often very difficult for young children to understand. The practical experience of using real objects to create a model facilitates understanding of this concept without any difficulty.

Bead activities

- Threading beads is one of the oldest and most effective ways of teaching children to work from left to right.
- The instructions on the activity sheets specify the order in which the beads must be threaded.
- These activities will promote the skill of sequencing, which is vital for reading and writing.
- Sequencing is very important in math once children start working with units—tens, hundreds, and thousands—a number in a sequence has a different value when it is placed in a different position.
- Children have to select (by sorting and matching) and then sequence the beads into the correct order.
- Fine motor skills and eye-hand coordination will be practiced in every activity.

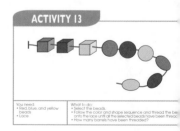

ACTIVITY BOOK

Card activities

- At the preschool age, children are anxious to participate in games with older children.
- Card games are a wonderful way to introduce the youngsters to social rules.
- No one can win every game—every child needs to learn how to lose.
- Waiting for one's turn is not always fun, but it is a skill that every child has to learn.
- While learning these social skills, children practice number, sequencing, and matching skills.

Spinner activities

- The spinner with printed paper templates can be used on its own or combined with the other components.
- This component introduces the concept of chance and probability—a math skill that will also be used for estimation activities at a more advanced level.
- Encourage children to develop their own games.

How the activities help your child

- When parents do not know what their children need to learn, they cannot expose them to the appropriate activities and stimulation.
- A short explanation of the specific skills children develop when they complete each activity will help the parent to see where children need to improve.
- Read the instructions and explain them. Make sure the child knows what is expected of him or her.
- Ask questions about the activity and components and pay additional attention to extending vocabulary and descriptive language.
- Praise your child's efforts. Make use of the stars that have been included to recognize and reward good work.

Activity 1
Sort the beads according to color and shape. Repeat the sequence. Reinforce correct names (sphere, cube, cylinder, and barrel).

Activity 2
Make pairs and learn the names of the colors.

Activity 3
Practice sorting, matching, and grouping. Develop the skill of one-to-one correspondence in the process.

Activity 4
Discover that the four small blue squares put together are the same size as the large yellow square.

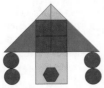

Activity 5
Practice sorting, matching, and grouping.

Activity 6
Apply one-to-one correspondence with shape and color.

Activity 7
Practice sorting, matching, and grouping shapes and colors.

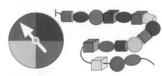

Activity 8
Sequencing so many cubes is challenging for a small child. Encourage children to complete the activity.

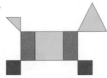

ACTIVITY BOOK

Activity 9
Select, match, and discard. The activity will sharpen visual discrimination skills.

Activity 10
Are children able to remember the pattern without looking at the illustration all the time? Visual memory will systematically improve.

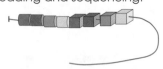

Activity 11
Are children able to select the correct shapes and colors?

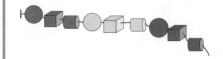

Activity 12
Build from top to bottom. Are the finger muscles strong enough to push the cubes together?

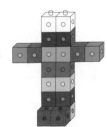

Activity 13
Are children improving their speed at selecting the correct beads?

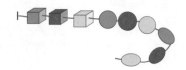

Activity 14
It takes good planning to put all the cubes in the correct positions.

Activity 15
A copying activity where some shapes must be placed on top of and next to other shapes to create this design.

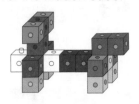

Activity 16
Investigate and apply reasoning to discover the hidden cube.

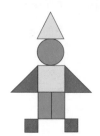

Activity 17
Is the child's technique improving when building? If the construction is breaking while building, push the cubes tighter into each other.

Activity 18
Practice fine motor skills and eye-hand coordination. Practice shape and color recognition.

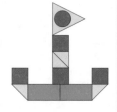

Activity 19
Application of analysis and synthesis while improving observation skills.

Activity 20
Are children starting to make use of visual memory? Show the illustration to your child for only a few minutes, then let him or her rely on visual memory.

Activity 21
Develop visual memory skills while threading and sequencing.

Activity 22
Can the child apply the triangles in the different positions? Is the child rotating and flipping the shapes to create the design?

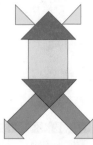

Activity 23
Application of spatial relationship and copying skills.

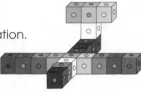

Activity 24
A more challenging design that requires increased concentration.

Activity 25
Practice sorting skills.

Activity 26
Enhance spatial relationship skills. The child may observe that several different shapes, when combined, create new shapes that are all equal in size (early experiences with fractions).

ACTIVITY BOOK

Activity 27
Experience with part/whole relationship while discovering new shapes.

Activity 28
Develop spatial relationship skills. Rotate and flip the shapes into the correct positions to build the design.

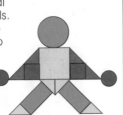

Activity 29
Read the instructions only once to see how well your child listens. Challenge the auditory memory.

Activity 30
Shape activities stimulate planning and thinking skills.

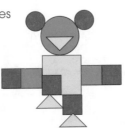

Activity 31
A concrete activity to introduce basic fractions. The child will become aware that different shapes can be modified to create new shapes that are equal in size.

Activity 32
Match quantity to numerals.

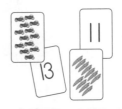

Activity 33
Concrete experiences with shape and size. Develop fine motor and sequencing skills.

Activity 34
Challenging spatial relationship skills and logical thinking. Children begin to understand the application of position and space.

Activity 35
Develop visual memory skills and apply what has been learned about shape and color.

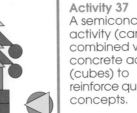

Activity 36
Application of shape to practice one-to-one correspondence and understanding foreground/background.

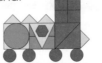

Activity 37
A semiconcrete activity (cards) combined with a concrete activity (cubes) to reinforce quantity concepts.

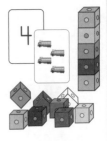

Activity 38
Ask children to describe the positions of the individual shapes. Can they use terms such as *next to, on top, below*, etc.?

Activity 39
Discover how shapes can be used to build other designs.

Activity 40
Develop understanding of fundamental math terminology such as *above, below*, and *between*.

Activity 41
Can children describe the positions of the individual shapes? Do they know the terms *next to, on top,* and *below*?

Activity 42
Reinforce positional understanding and positional language.

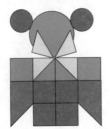

Activity 43
Apply one-to-one correspondence and visual perception skills.

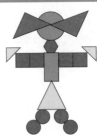

Activity 44
Practice fine motor skills and visual perception skills.

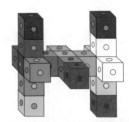

ACTIVITY BOOK

Activity 45
Practice positional awareness and mathematical vocabulary.

Activity 46
Understanding spatial relationships and fractions.

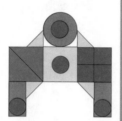

Activity 47
Making shape designs requires precise placing and reinforces fine motor skills and eye-hand coordination.

Activity 48
Practice following instructions to reach the desired outcome.

Activity 49
Reinforce positional understanding and positional language.

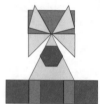

Activity 50
Apply one-to-one correspondence and advanced fine motor skills development.

Activity 51
Apply one-to-one correspondence that creates a pattern of yellow, blue, and red. Extends to a quantity activity.

Activity 52
A challenging activity in which children must think about where to position the cube in order to attach other cubes.

Activity 53
Develop fine motor and eye-hand coordination skills. Also a counting exercise.

Activity 54
A threading exercise to stimulate fine motor development and shape recognition.

Activity 55
A fun card activity that improves addition and number skills.

Activity 56
Requires the use of observation and counting skills to answer the questions.

Activity 57
Apply creative thinking and reinforce one-to-one correspondence skills.

Activity 58
Introduction to multiplication by threading groups of 4.

Activity 59
Discover symmetry and apply reasoning skills to build the spider.

Activity 60
Discover the relationship between different sizes and shapes.

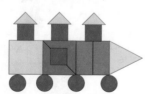

Activity 61
Find the correct positions to apply the shapes and practice spatial relation skills.

Activity 62
A challenging card game in which semiconcrete and abstract numbers are combined, improving matching and number skills. Explain the rules before the game starts.

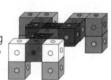

WORKBOOK

Once the child is comfortable with the components and can do the activities with little or no assistance, the workbook should be introduced.

The worksheets progress from very basic to more complex tasks. It is important to follow the sheets in sequence.

Coloring pencils or color markers are needed to complete some of the worksheets.

Read the instructions of each worksheet to your child before he or she starts.

All the worksheets have examples to follow.

Do not allow children to work with the workbook without understanding what is expected from them. Should a child encounter an activity that is not understood, he or she may get discouraged very easily.

Ask questions about the worksheet and pay additional attention to extending vocabulary and descriptive language as children progress.

It is important to give feedback to your child. Make use of the reward stars that have been included to recognize and reward good work.

WORKSHEET 1
Quantity 1–2

Count how many eyes, ears, arms and legs the teddy bear has. Complete and color the drawing.

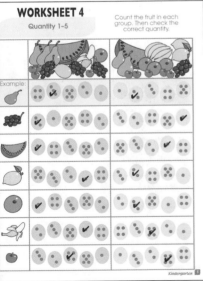

WORKSHEET 2
Quantity 1–3

Complete the picture so it includes three fish of each color.

WORKSHEET 3
Quantity 1–5

Count each kind of animal. Then check the box with the correct amount of dots.

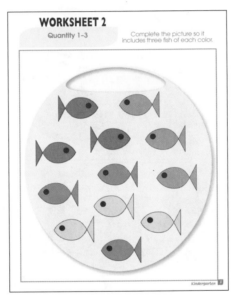

WORKSHEET 4
Quantity 1–5

Count the fruit in each group. Then check the correct quantity.

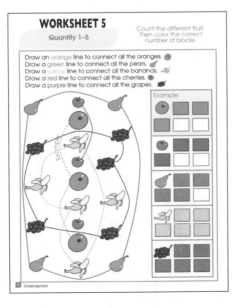

WORKSHEET 5
Quantity 1–5

Count the different fruit. Then color the correct number of blocks.

Draw an orange line to connect all the oranges.
Draw a green line to connect all the pears.
Draw a yellow line to connect all the bananas.
Draw a red line to connect all the cherries.
Draw a purple line to connect all the grapes.

WORKSHEET 6
Recording data

Count and record the colors by drawing the same number of dots.

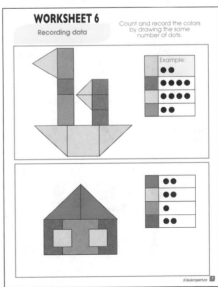

WORKSHEET 7
Recording data — Count and record the shapes by drawing the same number of dots.

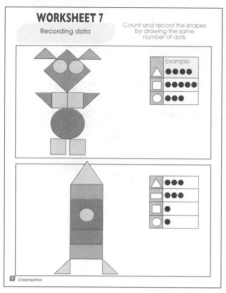

WORKSHEET 8
Sequence and color — Complete the patterns by coloring the shapes.

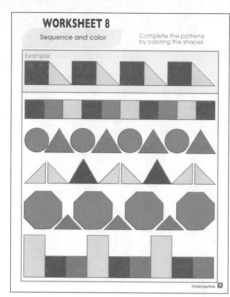

WORKSHEET 9
Recording data — Count the shapes of each color. Then record the number of each with a check mark.

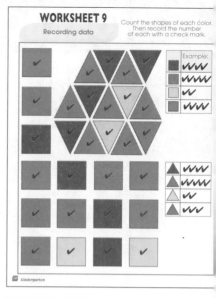

WORKSHEET 10
Sorting and counting — Count each kind of animal and record by circling the correct amount of dots.

WORKSHEET 11
Spot the differences — Circle five things in the bottom picture that are different from the top picture.

WORKSHEET 12
Numbers 1–5 — Count the fingers being held up. Follow the arrows and complete the numbers.

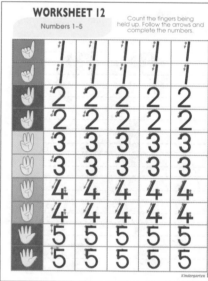

WORKSHEET 13
Quantity 1–5 — Count the pictures. Draw the same number of dots and write the number.

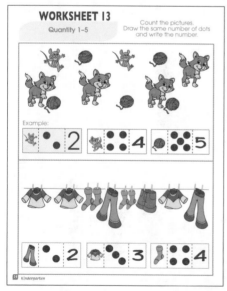

WORKSHEET 14
Ordinal numbers — Follow the instructions below.

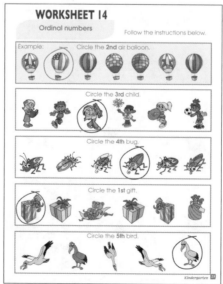

Example: Circle the **2nd** air balloon.
Circle the **3rd** child.
Circle the **4th** bug.
Circle the **1st** gift.
Circle the **5th** bird.

WORKSHEET 15
Count and color — How many objects do you see? Draw the same number of dots. Color the correct number.

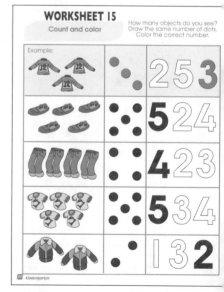

WORKSHEET 16
Spot the differences
Circle five things in the bottom picture that are different from the top picture.

WORKSHEET 17
Greater, less, or equal
Count the objects and use the correct symbols to show greater than, less than, or equal to.

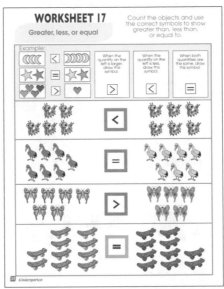

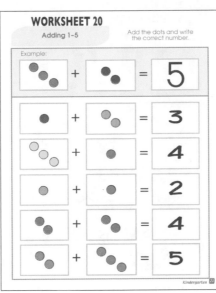

WORKSHEET 18
Numbers 1–5
Follow the arrows and complete the numbers.

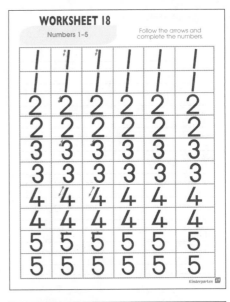

WORKSHEET 19
Adding 1–5
Count the flowers and draw the same number of dots. Add them up and write the correct number.

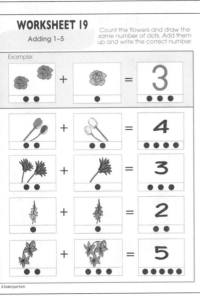

WORKSHEET 20
Adding 1–5
Add the dots and write the correct number.

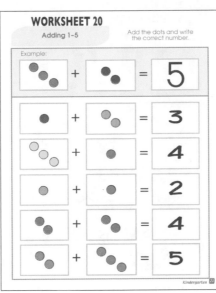

WORKSHEET 21
☀Day or ☾night
Indicate if these activities usually take place during the day or at night.

WORKSHEET 22
Matching pictures
Circle one item in each row that matches the one at the top.

WORKSHEET 23
Association
Draw lines to connect the appropriate gear to the activity.

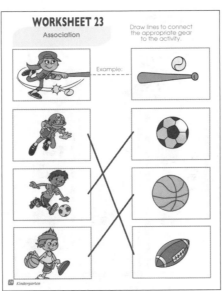

WORKSHEET 24
Heavy or light
Compare the pictures.

Check the box with the heavier item.

Check the box with the lighter object.

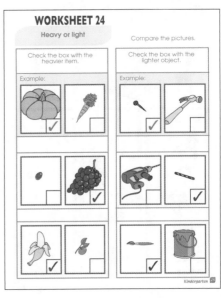

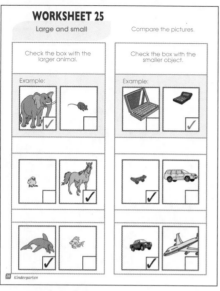

WORKSHEET 25
Large and small   Compare the pictures.

Check the box with the larger animal.

Check the box with the smaller object.

Example:

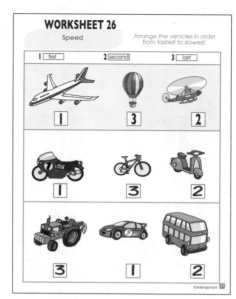

WORKSHEET 26
Speed   Arrange the vehicles in order from fastest to slowest.

1 first   2 second   3 last

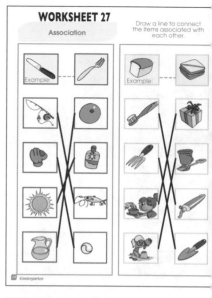

WORKSHEET 27
Association   Draw a line to connect the items associated with each other.

Example:

WORKSHEET 28
Classification   Circle the object that does not belong in each group.

Example:

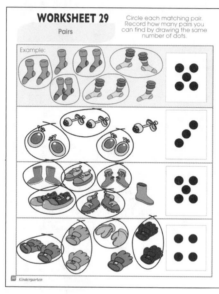

WORKSHEET 29
Pairs   Circle each matching pair. Record how many pairs you can find by drawing the same number of dots.

Example:

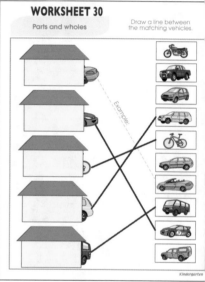

WORKSHEET 30
Parts and wholes   Draw a line between the matching vehicles.

Example:

WORKSHEET 31
Sort and classify   Draw lines to help the lost animals get to the groups where they belong.

Example:

Farm animals   Fish   Birds

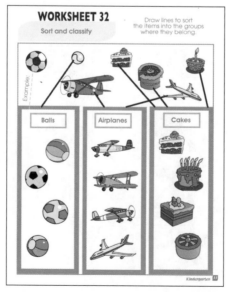

WORKSHEET 32
Sort and classify   Draw lines to sort the items into the groups where they belong.

Example:

Balls   Airplanes   Cakes

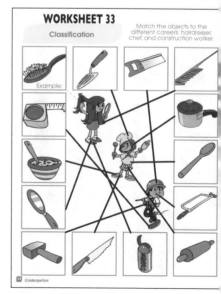

WORKSHEET 33
Classification   Match the objects to the different careers: hairdresser, chef, and construction worker.

Example:

WORKSHEET 34

Classification

Sort the items into the correct group.

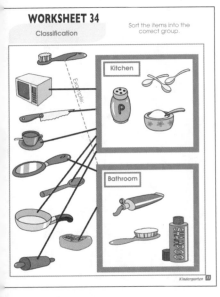

WORKSHEET 35

Classification

Draw a line from each group of ingredients to the correct food or drink.

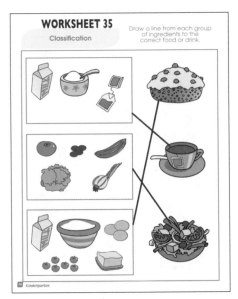

WORKSHEET 36

Ordering

Arrange the pictures in the order in which they happened by using the numbers 1, 2, and 3.

| 1 first | 2 second | 3 last |

Example:

WORKSHEET 37

Adding 1–5

Add the sums and write the correct number.

Example:

$2 + 1 = 3$ $2 + 2 = 4$

$3 + 2 = 5$ $0 + 3 = 3$

$1 + 3 = 4$ $3 + 1 = 4$

$1 + 1 = 2$ $2 + 3 = 5$

$4 + 1 = 5$ $2 + 0 = 2$

$4 + 0 = 4$ $0 + 5 = 5$

WORKSHEET 38

Numbers 6–10

Count the fingers being held up. Follow the arrows and complete the numbers.

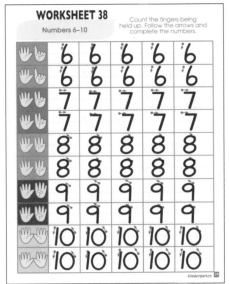

WORKSHEET 39

Direction and quantity 6–10

Count the objects and check the correct number of dots. Check the arrow that matches the direction in which the objects are moving.

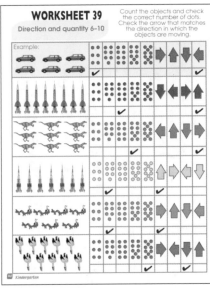

WORKSHEET 40

Adding 1–10

Add the numbers and write the answers.

Example:

$2 + 3 = 5$ $4 + 1 = 5$

$2 + 1 = 3$ $1 + 3 = 4$

$7 + 2 = 9$ $0 + 9 = 9$

$6 + 2 = 8$ $1 + 5 = 6$

$6 + 0 = 6$ $5 + 2 = 7$

WORKSHEET 41

Quantity and numbers 6–10

Count the dots and then circle the same number of objects. Write the correct number.

Example:

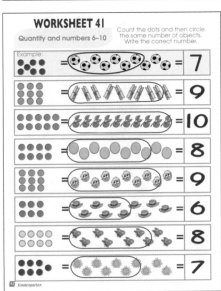

WORKSHEET 42

Adding 1–10

Add the dots and write the correct number.

Example:

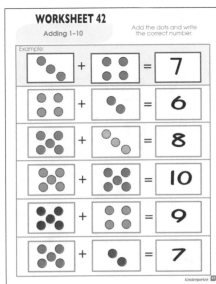

WORKSHEET 43

Quantity and numbers 6–10

Count the objects and circle the correct number.

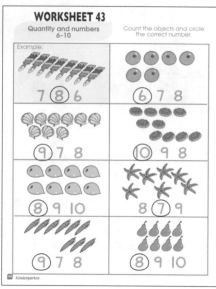

WORKSHEET 44

Addition 6–10

Count and add the objects. Write the correct number.

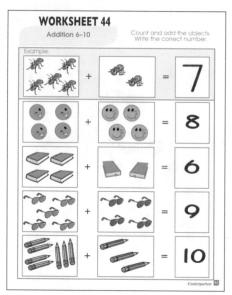

WORKSHEET 45

Addition

Add the objects and write the correct number.

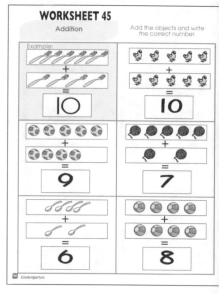

WORKSHEET 46

Numbers 6–10

Follow the arrows and complete the numbers.

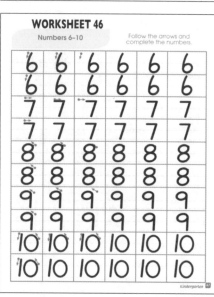

WORKSHEET 47

Adding 1–10

Add the numbers and write the answers.

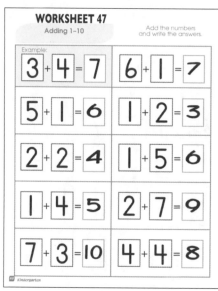

WORKSHEET 48

Matching

Circle the picture that matches the one on the left.

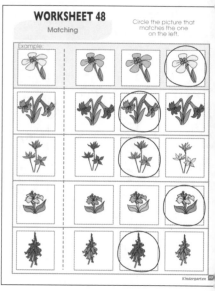

WORKSHEET 49

Combinations

Circle the set of shapes that matches the one on the left.

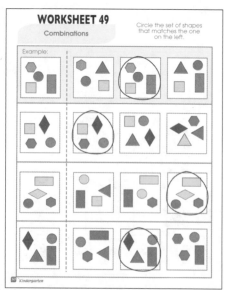

WORKSHEET 50

Combinations

Circle the set of shapes that matches the one on the left.

WORKSHEET 51

Combinations

Circle the set of objects that matches the one on the left.

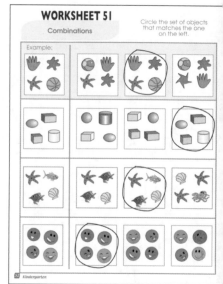